I0005271

NODE. JS

PRACTICAL GUIDE FOR

BEGINNERS

Third Edition, Revised and Enlarged

By Matthew Gimson

Table of Contents

Disclaimer

While all attempts have been made to verify the information provided in this book, the author does assume any responsibility for errors, omissions, or contrary interpretations of the subject matter contained within. **The information provided in this book is for educational and entertainment purposes only. The reader is responsible for his or her own actions and the author does not accept any responsibilities for any liabilities or damages, real or perceived, resulting from the use of this information.**

The trademarks that are used are without any consent, and the publication of the trademark is without permission or backing by the trademark owner. All trademarks and brands within this book are for clarifying purposes only and are the owned by the owners themselves, not affiliated with this document.

Introduction

The Node.js platform, which is solely based on JavaScript, is well known for its strong support of both data-intensive and real-time apps. In the current world, this includes the majority of applications that are in use. This is why you need to know how to use this platform. This book will guide you in building of a strong understanding of this platform.

Chapter 1- Definition

Node.js is a platform that works on the server side of apps, and it was built in the JavaScript engine of Google Chrome. The aim of developing this platform is to help developers to easily build network applications that are fast and well scalable. The model used by this framework is a lightweight, non-blocking I/O, which explains its lightweight and efficient nature. When it comes to real time applications running across devices as well as those that utilize a substantial amount data, Node.js is the perfect platform. Keep in mind that this platform is a cross platform and its code is written in JavaScript. Its applications can be run in Windows, Linux, and OS X. With Node.js, numerous modules that belong to JavaScript are provided. This is why it is possible to expand these apps.

The APIs (Application Program Interface) for Node.js operates in a non-blocking manner, which means they do not wait for any data to be returned. The platform is also very fast when it comes to the execution of code. Event looping, using a single threaded model, is also supported. In addition, when it comes to buffering data, Node.js' applications do not do this. They only output data in chunks, and the platform was released under MIT license.

Chapter 2- Setting Up the Environment

If you need to perform a local environment setup, a text editor is needed together with the Node.js binary installable.

The Text Editor

The text editor will provide you with an environment in which you can type your program. Examples of common text editors include the Vim editor in Linux, the Notepad editor in Windows, and the EMACS editor in Mac OS X. Once you have created a file in one of these text editors, you can add your code to it and the file will be said to have the source code for your program. The source files, which contain Node.js' programs, should have a *.js* extension in their name. Note that the source files will contain JavaScript code, and the Node.js interpreter is used to interpret this source code for the program. Node.js can be installed on various operating systems, such as Linux, Windows, Mac OS X, and SunOS.

Begin by downloading the Node.js archive online, which is available for free download.

Installation on SunOS/Unix/Linux/Mac OS X

Once you have performed the download, extract the files into the **/usr/local/nodejs** directory. If you have already extracted these in a different directory, you can move the extracted files into this preferred directory. The following sequence of commands can be used for this purpose:

```
$ cd /tmp

$ wget http://nodejs.org/dist/v0.12.0/node-v0.12.0-linux-x64.tar.gz

$ tar xvfz node-v0.12.0-linux-x64.tar.gz

$ mkdir -p /usr/local/nodejs

$ mv node-v0.12.0-linux-x64/* /usr/local/nodejs
```

Note that we have begun by downloading the files for Node.js. After the download, we extracted the contents. We used the command **mkdir** to create a new directory. It is in this directory that we moved the extracted contents of the download. The directory **/usr/local/nodejs/bin** should then be added to the **PATH** environment variable.

Installation in Windows

In this case, you should use the *MSI* file for the installation process. You will follow prompts to install the program. By default, you will notice that the installer will install the program in the directory *C:\Program Files\nodejs*. Once you have completed the installation, you should restart all of the command prompts that are open, so that the changes can be applied.

Once you are done, verify the installation to ensure it ran successfully. Create a file and give it the name *test.js*. Once you have created the file, add the following code to it:

/* Hello! program in node.js */
console.log("Hello, welcome to Node.js!")

Once you have written the program, run it by opening the terminal and executing the following command:

node test.js

If everything ran correctly during installation, then you should observe the following result:

```
Hello, welcome to Node.js!
```

Chapter 3- Global Objects in Node.js

The global objects in Node.js can be accessed globally, meaning that they are accessible from all modules. If you need to use these objects inside your program, you won't have to include them inside your program, but you can use them directly. The objects in this case include: modules, strings, functions, and the object itself.

These are discussed below:

_filename

This is used to represent the name of the file of the code that is to be executed. It represents the resolved absolute path of the code file. This should not be the filename used in the command line. The value provided inside a module should be the path leading to the module file. Consider the example given below:

Create a file named *file.js* and then add the following code to it:

//We need to print the value of ___filename
console.log(___filename);

Once you have added the code to the file, run it. You will notice the value of the _*filename*. You should give it a name that resembles the following:

/web/com/2327083027_21786/main.js

_dirname

When this is used, it represents the directory in which the current script in execution resides. Create a file named *file.js* and add the following code to it:

// We need to print the value of __dirname

console.log(__dirname);

Once you have added the code to the file, save the file and run it by executing the following command on the terminal:

$ node file.js

You will observe the following output:

Note that the result may not be similar, as it is determined by where you have saved your file.

setTimeout(cb, ms)

This is a global function that programmers use to run the callback (cb) after the expiry of the ms milliseconds. Factors such as the granularity of the system and the system load will determine the actual delay in terms of milliseconds. Note that it is impossible for a timer to span for over 24.8 days.

The value returned by this function is an opaque one, and it stands for the timer you can use to clear the timer. Let us demonstrate this by use of an example:

Create a file named *file.js,* and then add the following code to it:

function sayHello(){
      console.log("Hello, there!");
}
// the above function can then be called after 2 seconds

setTimeout(sayHello, 2000);

Execute the above program and observe the output that you get. It should be as follows:

```
Hello, there!
```

clearTimeout(t)

This function is used for stopping a time you created recently. The timer is created by use of the function *setTimeOut()*. The parameter *t* represents the timer that is to be returned by the *setTimeout()* function. Let us demonstrate this by use of an example.

Create a file named *file.js* and then add the following code to it:

```
function sayHello(){
        console.log( "Hello, there!");
}
// You can then call the above function after 2
seconds
var t = setTimeout(sayHello, 2000);
```

```
// You can then clear the timer
      clearTimeout(t);
```

Once you have written the program, run it. You will observe the following:

```
Hello, there!
```

The timer was set to execute the function after 2 seconds (2000 milliseconds), and the name of the function is "sayHello()". After that, the timer has been cleared using the "clearTimeout(t)" function.

setInterval(cb, ms)

This method is used to run the **cb** after every **ms**. External factors, such as the system load and the OS timer granularity, will determine the actual delay of the system. This function also returns an opaque value. Let us demonstrate this by use of an example.

Create a new file and give it the name **file.js**. Add the following code to it:

function sayHello(){

```
        console.log( "Hello, there!");
}
```
// You can then call the above function after 2 seconds

```
        setInterval(sayHello, 2000);
```

Run the program and observe the output. It should be as follows:

```
Hello, there!
```

Chapter 4- Utility Modules in Node.js

The Node.js module library provides a number of utilities for programmers. Programmers then use them whenever they are developing applications that are related to Node.js. Let us discuss some of these modules:

OS Module

This module provides us with some utility functions that are related to the operating system. To import this module in Node.js, the following syntax is used:

var os = require("os")

This module provides a number of utilities that are related to the operating system. We need to demonstrate how this can be done.

Create a new file and give it the name *file.js*. Add the following code to the file:

var myos = require("os");
// Endianness
      console.log('endianness : ' +
myos.endianness());

```
// getting the OS type
        console.log('type : ' + myos.type());
// The OS platform
        console.log('The     platform    :    '    +
myos.platform());
// The Total system memory
        console.log('The    total    memory    :    '    +
myos.totalmem() + " bytes.");

// The Total free memory
        console.log('The    free    memory    :    '    +
myos.freemem() + " bytes.");
```

Once you have added the code to the file, run it and observe the output. It should be as follows:

```
endianness : LE
The type : Linux
The platform : linux
The total memory : 25103400960 bytes.
The free memory : 14904430592 bytes.
```

In the function "endianness()", we are getting the endianness of our CPU. This cna only give two values, that is, LE and BR, and in this case, we get "LE". The type() function should give us the type of operating system that is currently in use. In this case, we are using Linux, as shown in the above output. The platform is also Linux, as the above output shows. The totalmem() function gives us the total size of the memory in bytes. The amount of free memory has been obtained using the freemem() function.

The PATH Module

This module is used for transformation and handling of file paths. To import it, use the following syntax:

var **path** = require**("path")**

Let us demonstrate how this module can be used by use of an example.

Create a new file and then give it a name with a *.js* extension. Add the following code to the file:

```
var p = require("path");
// Normalization process
console.log('normalization : ' +
p.normalize('/usr/test//slashes/slash/programs/..'));

// Joining
console.log('joint path : ' + p.join('/usr', 'test',
'slashes/slash', 'programs', '..'));

// Resolve
console.log('The resolve : ' + p.resolve('file.js'));
// extName
console.log('The ext name : ' + p.extname('main.js'));
```

Once you have written the program, run it and observe the. It should be as follows:

```
The normalization : /usr/test/slashes/slash
joint path : /usr/test/slashes/slash
The resolve : /web/com/1439199994_1244/main.js
The exit name : .js
```

The function normalize() is used for joining the strings of a path name, and that is why we get a normalized path name in the above example. The resolve() function has given us an absolute path. The "extname() function usually returns the extension of the path name when it is used.

The "*Net*" Module

This module is used for creation of both the clients and the servers. To import it, use the following syntax:

var **n** = require**("net")**

Let us demonstrate how the module can be used by use of an example.

Create a new file and give it the name *file.js*. Add the following code to it:

```
var n = require('net');
var s = n.createServer(function(connection) {
        console.log('client has been connected');
        connection.on('end', function() {
                console.log('client has been
disconnected');
});
        connection.write('Hello there!\r\n');
        connection.pipe(connection);
});
s.listen(8080, function() {
        console.log('The server is listening');
});
```

Once you have added the code, run the program by opening the terminal and running the following command:

node file.js

The following output will be observed:

The server is listening

The above file has the code for the server. Now you will need to create a file with the client code. Open the text editor, create a new file, and give it the name *file2.js*. Add the following code to the file:

```
var n = require('net');
var cl = n.connect({port: 8080}, function() {
        console.log('Now connected to the server!');
});
cl.on('data', function(data) {
        console.log(data.toString());
        cl.end();
});
cl.on('end', function() {
        console.log('Now disconnected from the
server');
```

```
});
```

Once you have written the above code into the file, run it by executing the following command:

node file2.js

The following output will be observed:

> Now connected to the server!
>
> Hello there!
>
> Now disconnected from the server

The function net.createServer() has been used to create the TCP server. The function net.connect() has been used to establish a connection to the address that has been specified, that is, the port number 8080. The function "server.listen()" makes the server listen to the port 8080 for an incoming connection from the client.

The "*DNS*" Module

This module is intended to perform the actual lookup for the DNS (domain name system) as well as to use the resolution functionalities of the underlying operating system. Note that the module provides you with an asynchronous network wrapper. To import it, use the syntax given below:

var **dns** = require**("dns")**

Let us demonstrate how this module can be used.

Create a new file and give it the name *file.js*. Add the following code to the file:

```
var dns = require('dns');
dns.lookup('www.facebook.com', function
onLookup(error, addr, family) {

        console.log('addr:', addr);
dns.reverse(addr, function (error, hostnames) {
        if (error) {
                console.log(error.stack);
}
        console.log('The reverse for ' + addr + ': ' +
JSON.stringify(hostnames));

});
```

});

Once you have written the above code into the file, run it by executing the following command:

node file.js

You will observe:

```
addr: 173.252.88.66
The reverse for 173.252.88.66: ["edge-star-shv-03-atn1.facebook.com"]
```

In the above example, we are resolving the hostname facebook.com into the IPV4 or IPV6 address that is found first. This has been done using the "dns.lookup()" and "dns.onlookup()" functions. The result for this is shown above.

The "*Domain*" Module

This module for Node.js is used for interception of an error that has not been handled. To intercept errors, you can use either internal binding or external binding. If you do not handle the errors in your application, then your Node.js application will crash.

Internal binding- with this, the error emitter executes its code within the run method of a domain.

External binding- with this, the error emitter is explicitly added to the domain by use of its ***add*** method. To import this module, use the syntax given below:

var **domain** = require**("domain")**

This module provides the Domain class that is responsible for routing errors and the exceptions that have been caught to the domain object that is active. For it to handle the errors that have been caught, you have to listen to its error event. Create it by using the syntax given below:

var **domain** = require**("domain");**
var **child** = **domain.create();**

We now need to demonstrate how this module can be used. Create a new file and give it the name *file.js*. Add the following code to the file:

```
var EvEmitter = require("events").EventEmitter;
var dom = require("domain");
var em1 = new EventEmitter();
// Creating a domain
var dom1 = dom.create();
dom1.on('error', function(error){
        console.log("dom1 has handled this error
        ("+error.message+")");
});
// Binding explicitly
dom1.add(em1);
em1.on('error',function(error){
        console.log("The listener handled this error
("+error.message+")");
});
em1.emit('error',new Error('This is to be handled by
the listener'));

em1.removeAllListeners('error');
em1.emit('error',new Error('This is to be handled by
dom1'));
var dom2 = dom.create();
dom2.on('error', function(error){
```

```
        console.log("The dom2 handled this error
    error.message+")");

});
// Binding implicitly

dom2.run(function(){

var em2 = new EventEmitter();

em2.emit('error',new Error('This is to be handled by
the dom2'));

});
dom1.remove(em1);

em1.emit('error', new Error('It has been converted to
an exception. The system will crash!')); var
EventEmitter = require("events").EventEmitter;

var dom = require("domain");

var emit1 = new EventEmitter();

// Creating a dom
var dom1 = dom.create();

dom1.on('error', function(err){
  console.log("dom1 handled this error
("+err.message+")");
});

// Explicit binding
dom1.add(emit1);

emit1.on('error',function(err){
  console.log("listener handled this error
("+err.message+")");
});
```

```
emit1.emit('error',new Error('To be handled by
listener'));

emit1.removeAllListeners('error');

emit1.emit('error',new Error('To be handled by
dom1'));

var dom2 = dom.create();

dom2.on('error', function(err){
  console.log("dom2 handled this error
("+err.message+")");
});

// Implicit binding
dom2.run(function(){
  var emit2 = new EventEmitter();
  emit2.emit('error',new Error('To be handled by
dom2'));
});


dom1.remove(emit1);
emit1.emit('error', new Error('Converted to
exception. System will crash!'));
```

Write the above program as it is displayed here, and then run
it by executing the following command:

node file.js

You will then observe the following:

The listener handled this error   (This is to be handled by the listener)
dom1 has handled this error   (This is to be handled by dom1)
The dom2 handled this error   (This is to be handled by the dom2)

Chapter 5- The Web Module in Node.js

A web server is an application that is tasked with handling Http: requests from clients. The response to the request is in the form of web pages sent to the client.

Using Node to Create a Web Server

Node.js has a module named **http** that can be used to create either a HTTP server or client. We need to demonstrate how an HTTP server can be created with Node.js.

Create a new file and give it the name **server.js**. Add the following code to the file:

```
var h = require('http');
var f = require('fs');
var url = require('url');
// Creating a server
h.createServer( function (req, response) {
// Parsing the request having the file name
var pname = url.parse(req.url).pathname;
// Printing the name of the file for receiving the
request.
```

```
        console.log("The Request is for" + pname +
        "has been received.");

// Reading the content for the requested file from the
file system

f.readFile(pname.substr(1), function (error, data) {
if (error) {
        console.log(error);
// The HTTP Status: 404 : NOT FOUND
// Content Type: text/plain
        res.writeHead(404, {'Content-Type':
'text/html'});
}else{
//Page found
// HTTP Status: 200 : OK
// Content Type: text/plain
        res.writeHead(200, {'Content-Type':
'text/html'});
// Writing the file's content to the response body
        res.write(d.toString());
}
// Sending the response body
res.end();
});
}).listen(8081);
//The console will print message
```

```
        console.log('The    Server    is    running    at
http://127.0.0.1:8081/');
```

Once you have added the code to the file, save it. The code represents a server that will be listening to the port 8081. This is the port on the localhost, as specified above.

In the same directory where you created the above file, create a new file named *index.html*. Add the following code to it:

```
<html>
<head>
<title>This is our Page</title>
</head>
<body>
Hello there!
</body>
</html>
```

Once you have added the above code to the file, save it. We have just created an HTML page that will display the text "This is our Page".

You can then run the server file by executing the following command:

node server.js

The above command should start the server, meaning that it will begin to listen at the port 8081, waiting for the client to establish a connection.

Once you have executed the above code, you will get the following output:

The Server is running at http://127.0.0.1:8081/

The above output shows that your server is executing properly. Now send a request to the server from the client. The client is the web page, which has to be launched on the browser. Open the browser, and then enter the following URL:

http://127.0.0.1:8081/index.html

After entering the above URL, hit the **Return** key to see the output. You should get the following:

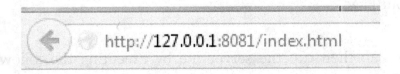

Hello there!

The output shows that our client code is okay and running as expected. You can also verify the output from the server side, and if all is well, you will be informed that the request from the client, that is, index.htm, was received.

Using Node.js to Create a Web Client

The *http* module can be used for creation of a web client in Node.js. Let us demonstrate how this can be done.

Open your text editor and create a new file named *client.js*. Add the following code to the file:

```
var h = require('http');
// Options which the request will use
var opts = {
host: 'localhost',
port: '8081',
path: '/index.html'
};
// The Callback function used for dealing with the
response
var cback = function(res){
// updating the stream continuously with data
var bd = '';
res.on('data', function(data) {
bd += data;
});
res.on('end', function() {
// The Data was received completely.
```

```
console.log(bd);
});
}
// Making a request to server
var req = h.request(opts, cback);
req.end();
```

Note that we have defined the options that our client is to use. We have also defined a callback function, that is, cback, and this will be tasked with dealing with the response. We have defined an object named "req" so as to make a request to the server. Now open another terminal. Run the above program in the new terminal as follows:

```
node client.js
<html>
<head>
<title>This is our Page</title>
</head>
<body>
Hello there!
</body>
</html>
```

The output should then be verified at the server end. You should get the following:

The Server is running at http://127.0.0.1:8081/

The Request is for /index.html has been received.");

The output shows that the server has received the client request and that all is working well.

Chapter 6- The REPL Terminal

The REPL (Read Eval Print Loop) is a terminal or a command prompt like the one for Windows and Linux. It accepts commands that are entered by the user, and it then provides output to the user in an interactive mode. Note that the Node.js comes with this terminal already installed.

This terminal is useful to debug JavaScript codes and for experimentation with codes belonging to Node.js.

Once you have installed Node.js on your system, you will need to access the REPL terminal by running the following command:

Node

After running the above command, you should be presented with the command prompt for REPL, which is the greater than symbol (>).

Performing Mathematics on the REPL Terminal

With the REPL terminal, you are able to perform simple mathematics. On the command prompt for REPL, execute the following expression:

10 + 10

Type the above command, and then hit the **_Return_** key. You will observe the following:

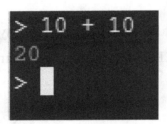

The expression gives us the result of adding 10 and 10, which is 20. Note that the REPL terminal is capable of observing the BODMAS (Brackets of Division, Multiplication, Addition and Subtraction) rule. To demonstrate this, run the following expression:

5 + (4 * 4) − 2

Once you have typed the command, hit the Return key, and then observe what happens. The following output should be observed:

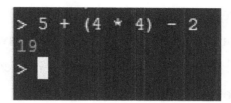

As shown in the obtained output, the Node.js interpreter first worked on the brackets, followed by the addition, and then the subtraction. This explains the source of the output shown in the above figure and the BODMAS rule was obeyed.

Use of Variables on the REPL Terminal

When variables are used, values are stored in them, and they are printed later. In this case, use the **var** keyword. In any case this keyword is not used, the value you have stored will be printed immediately. When this keyword is used, you can print the value of the variable at the time that you want. To do the printing, ***use console.log()***. Consider the example below:

```
> p = 10
10
> var q = 30
undefined
> p + q
40
> console.log( "This is the REPL terminal")
This is the REPL terminal
undefined
>
```

As shown in the above output, in the first line, that is, p = 10, the integer was returned immediately since we did not use the "var" keyword. In the next declaration, that is, var q = 30, the keyword "undefined" has been returned but not the value of the variable. This is because we have used the "var" keyword in the declaration or definition of the variable. You have to choose either of these depending on what you expect or need.

Multiline Expressions

Like in JavaScript, multiline expressions are supported in the REPL terminal. Let us execute a loop on the REPL terminal.

```
> var a = 0
undefined
> do {
... a++;
... console.log("The value of a is:" + a);
... }
... while (a < 7);
The value of a is:1
The value of a is:2
The value of a is:3
The value of a is:4
The value of a is:5
The value of a is:6
The value of a is:7
undefined
>
```

As shown in the figure above, begin by declaring a variable *a*, initialize its value to *0* (zero). Increase the increment of this value from zero up to 7, and you will see how this has been done. Once you have pressed the Return key, you will notice that you are taken to the next line until you have closed the loop and indicated the condition. This is how the terminal supports multiline expressions. Notice that the symbol *"..."* comes automatically once you have pressed the Return key.

The Node also has the capability of looking for continuity of the expressions.

The Variable Underscore

The underscore variable (_) is used to get the last result. Consider the example given below:

```
> var p = 1
undefined
> var q = 2
undefined
> q - p
1
> var difference = _
undefined
> console.log(difference)
1
undefined
>
```

As you can see in the above figure, difference between the two variables was obtained, which forms the last result. Use the underscore variable to print this out. We have defined a variable named "difference", and the value of this variable has been set to be the last result of our previous calculation, and this should be 1. Lastly, we have used "console.log" to print the value of this variable on the terminal.

Now you know how to perform numerous tasks with the REPL terminal. However, it is good for you to know some of its commands, especially the keyboard shortcuts. These are discussed below:

- ctrl + d – used to terminate the Node REPL.

- ctrl + c – used to terminate the current command.

- Up/Down Keys – used for viewing the command history and modifying previous commands.

- tab Keys – used for listing of the current commands.

- .break – used to exit from the multiline expression.

- .load *filename* – used to load file content in the current Node REPL session.

- .help – used for listing all commands.

- .clear – used to exit from the multiline expression.

- .save *filename* – used to save the current Node REPL session to a certain file.

- ctrl + c twice – used to terminate the Node REPL.

How to Stop the REPL Terminal

If you need to quit the REPL terminal, you will press the keys "*Ctrl + c*" twice, and you will exit. You are now familiar with how to perform the various tasks with the REPL terminal. This is demonstrated below:

$ node

>

(^C again to quit)

>

Chapter 7- Scaling an Application in Node.js

Node.js usually runs in a single thread mode. However, for handling concurrency, an event-driven approach is used. Creation of parallel processes is also facilitated for leveraging of parallel processing on systems that have a multi-core CPU.

Each child usually has three streams, which include child.stdout, child.stdin and child.stderr.

The *"exec()"* Method

This command is used for running a particular command on the shell, and then it buffers the output for the command. This method uses the syntax given below:

child_process.exec(command[, options], callback)

The "command" specifies the string that is to be run by the command, and its arguments are separated using a space. The arguments for the options can be cwd, env, encoding, shell, timeout, maxBuffer, killSignal, uid or gid. The callback function should take only three arguments, that is, error, stdout, and stderr. This method will return the buffer with a maximum size. It will then wait for the process to end. All the data that was buffered will then be returned at once. See below for a demonstration on how this method can be used.

Open your text editor, and then create a new file and give it the name *file1.js*. Add the following code to the file:

```
console.log("The child Process " + process.argv[2] + " is being executed." );
```

Again, create a new file and give it the name *file2.js*. Add the following code to the file:

```
const f = require('fs');

const cprocess = require('child_process');


for(var i=0; i<3; i++) {

   var workerProcess = cprocess.exec('node support.js '+i,function

     (error, stdout, stderr) {
```

```
if (error) {

    console.log(error.stack);

    console.log('Error code: '+error.code);

    console.log('Signal received: '+error.signal);

}

console.log('stdout: ' + stdout);

console.log('stderr: ' + stderr);

});


workerProcess.on('exit', function (code) {

    console.log('The exit code for the child process is '+code);

});

}
```

Once you have added the above code to the file, run it, and then observe the output you receive. The following should be its first section:

```
The exit code for the child process is 127
The exit code for the child process is 127
The exit code for the child process is 127
```

The output above is made up of the exit code of the child process. The second part of the output will be as follows:

```
The Error code is :: 127
The signal was received:  null
The stdout:
The stderr: /bin/sh: The: command not found
```

The "*spawn()*" Method

This method is used for launching a new process, but with a new command. It takes the syntax given below:

child_process.spawn(command[, args][, options])

The "command" is the string that the command will run. The "args" refers to a list of arguments placed in an array. The value for the "options" can be cwd, env, stdio, customFds, detached, uid or gid. The method usually returns streams, that is, stdout and stderr. If you are expecting your process to return large amounts of data, then just use this method. Once the process has begun execution, the spawn() method will begin to receive responses immediately. When this method is used, streams are returned. You are encouraged to use this method when a large amount of data is returned. Once the execution of the process has begun, this method will begin to receive a response. See below to find a demonstration of how this method can be used.

Create a file named *file1.js,* and then add the following code to it:

console.log("The Child Process " + process.argv[2] + " has been executed.");

Create another file, and then give it the name *file2.js*. Add the following code to the file:

```
const f = require('fs');
const cprocess = require('child_process');
for(var j=0; j<3; j++) {
var wProcess = cprocess.spawn('node', ['file1.js', j]);
wProcess.stdout.on('data', function (data) {
        console.log('The stdout: ' + data);
});
wProcess.stderr.on('data', function (data) {
        console.log('The stderr: ' + data);
});
wProcess.on('close', function (code) {
        console.log('The child process exited with the code ' + code);

});
}
```

Once you have added the above code, run the second file by typing the following command in the terminal:

node file2.js

You will observe the following output after executing the above command:

```
The stdout: Child Process 0 executed.

The child process exited with the code child process exited with code 0
The stdout: Child Process 2 executed.

The stdout: Child Process 1 executed.

The child process exited with the code child process exited with code 0
The child process exited with the code child process exited with code 0
```

The *"fork"* Method

This is a special case of the *"spawn()"* method and is used for creation of Node processes. It requires the following syntax:

child_process.fork(modulePath[, args][, options])

The "modulePath" is the string which the module will run in the child. "The args" refers to a string of arguments placed in an array. The value for the options can be cwd, env, execPath, execArgv, silent, uid or gid. The return type of the *"fork"* method is an object having a built-in communication channel and it has all the methods in a normal instance of the child process.

See below to find a demonstration of how this method can be used in Node.js.

Create two files in your text editor. Name them *file1.js* and *file2.js*. Add the following code to *file1.js*:

console.log("Child Process " + process.argv[2] + " executed.");

Open the file *file2.js*, and then add the following code to it:

```javascript
const f = require('fs');
const cprocess = require('child_process');
for(var j = 0; j<3; j++) {
        var wprocess = cprocess.fork("support.js",
[j]);
        wprocess.on('close', function (code) {
        console.log('The child process exited with the
code ' + code);
});
}
```

You can then execute the file *file2.js* by executing the following command:

node file2.js

Observe the output that you get from the file. It should be as shown below:

```
Child Process 0 executed.
Child Process 1 executed.
Child Process 2 executed.
The child process exited with the code  0
The child process exited with the code  0
The child process exited with the code  0
```

The above is the output from the method.

Chapter 8- Streams in Node.js

Streams are a kind of objects. With them, you can read from a certain source or write to a certain destination. This can be done in a continuous manner. Node.js supports four types of streams. These include the following:

- Readable – This stream is used to perform a read operation.

- Writable – This stream is used to perform a write operation.

- Duplex – This stream can be used to perform both a read and a write operation.

- Transform – This is a kind of a duplex stream where the output is calculated based on the input.

A stream is a kind of an instance of an EventEmitter, and with it, several events are thrown at different instances of time.

Reading from a Stream

Continue on to find a demonstration of how to read from a certain stream.

Begin by opening your text editor, and then create a new text file. Give it the name *textfile.txt*. Add the following text to the file:

Streams are a kind of objects and with them you can read from a certain source or write to a certain destination. This can be done in a continuous manner.

Once you are done, create a new JS file and give it the name *file.js*. Add the following code to the JS file:

```
var f = require("fs");
var d = ";
// creating a stream which is readable
var rStream = f.createReadStream('textfile.txt');
// Setting the encoding to utf8.
rStream.setEncoding('UTF8');
// Handling the stream events --> d, end, and error
rStream.on('data', function(chunk) {
```

```
d += chunk;
});
rStream.on('end',function(){
        console.log(d);
});
rStream.on('error', function(error){
        console.log(error.stack);
});
        console.log("The Program has Ended");
```

Now that you have added the code to your file, it's time to run it. Open the terminal, and then execute the following command:

node file.js

Once you have executed the above command, you will get the following output:

The Program has Ended

Streams are a kind of objects and with them, one can read from a certain source or

to a certain destination and this can be done in a continuous manner.

We have created a reader stream object named "rStream", which has been used for reading the data from our text file. Note how the name of the text file to be read has been specified in the Node.js code. The program ended once it had read all the contents of the text file. That is why we had the file contents printed on the screen.

Writing to a Stream

To demonstrate how writing to a stream can be done follow the steps below.

Create a new text file named *file.js*, and then add the following code to it:

```
var f = require("fs");
var data = 'Streams are a kind of objects';
// Creating a stream which is writable
var wStream = f.createWriteStream('textfile.txt');
// Writing the data to a stream with the encoding
being utf8
wStream.write(data,'UTF8');
// Marking the end of the file
wStream.end();
// Handling the stream events finish, and error
wStream.on('finish', function() {
console.log("The Writing to the stream has completed.");
});
wStream.on('error', function(error){
console.log(error.stack);
});
console.log("The Program has Ended");
```

Once the above code has been added to the file, you can run it by executing the following command on the terminal:

node file.js

After executing the above command, you will get the following output:

> The Program has Ended
>
> The Writing to the stream has completed.

If you observe the above output, then everything should be okay. You should then verify whether the writing ran successfully. Navigate to your directory, and then open the file *textfile.txt*, and then verify the contents. They should be as follows:

Streams are a kind of objects

We created a variable named "data" for holding the data that is to be writtten to a text file named "textfile.txt". Once the write operation is completed, we get the message that the stream was written.

Stream Piping

With piping in streams, the output from a particular stream is made the input to another stream. Use this when you want to get data from a particular stream, and then pass the same data to the next stream in the chain. Note that the piping operation does not have a limit. The demonstration below will show how this can be done by giving an example in which data from a particular stream will be read, and then written to another stream.

Create a new file, and then give it the name *file.js*. Add the following code to the file:

```
var f = require("fs");
// Creating a stream which is readable
var rStream = f.createReadStream('textfile1.txt');
// Creating a stream which is writable
var wStream = f.createWriteStream('textfile2.txt');
// Piping the read and write operations
// reading the textfile1.txt and writing the data to
textfile2.txt
rStream.pipe(wStream);
console.log("The Program has Ended");
```

Once you have added the above code to the file, you can run it by executing the following command in the terminal:

node file.js

You should observe the following result after running the above command:

The Program has Ended

If you get the output shown in the above figure, you are successful. Navigate to the current directory, and then verify whether the file *textfile2.txt* was formed. If you find it, open it, and then verify the text it contains. It should be as follows:

Streams are a kind of objects and with them you can read from a certain source or write to a certain destination. This can be done in a continuous manner.

We created a variable named "rStream", which is a readable stream. This stream should read the text contained in the file "textfile1.txt". We have also created a writable stream named "wStream". This is to be used for writing the contents of the readable stream, rStream, into the "textfile2.txt". The data had to be piped from rStream to the wStream in the line "rStream.pipe(wStream);". That is, the second file was formed and data was written into it.

Chaining of Streams

What happens in stream chaining is that the output from a particular stream is connected to another stream and multiple stream operations are made. The chaining operation is used together with the piping operation. To demonstrate how this can be done, view the example below of how to use the piping and chaining operations to compress a particular file, and then decompress it. Create a file with the name *file.js,* and then add the following code to it:

```
var f = require("fs");
var compress = require('zlib');
// Compressing the file textfile.txt to textfile.txt.gz
f.createReadStream('textfile.txt')
.pipe(compress.createGzip())
.pipe(f.createWriteStream('textfile.txt.gz'));

        console.log("The File has been
Compressed.");
```

Once you have added the code to the file, run it by executing the following code:

```
node file.js
```

The above command should give you the following output:

```
The File has been Compressed.
```

You can navigate to your current directory and observe that the file **textfile.txt** has been compressed to **textfile.txt.gz**. Once a file has been compressed, the .gz extension is added to the file name. Now that the file has been compressed, you can use the following code:

var f = require("fs");
var compress = require('zlib');
// Decompressing the file textfile.txt.gz to textfile.txt
f.createReadStream('textfile.txt.gz')
.pipe(compress.createGunzip())
.pipe(f.createWriteStream('textfile.txt'));

console.log("The File has been Decompressed.");

Once you have added the above code to your file, use the following command to run it:

node file.js

The above command should give you the following output:

```
The File has been Compressed.
```

The above program works by uncompressing the file so as to get our normal text file. Note that once a file has been compressed, a number of changes are made to it, such as a reduction in size. To get our normal file, we have to uncompress it, as shown in the above code.

Chapter 9- The RESTful API in Node.js

REST (Representational State Transfer) is a web standard based architecture that uses the HTTP protocol. In this architecture, every component is a resource and access to a resource is done via the common interface by use of the HTTP standards method.

The purpose of the REST server is to provide access to the resources, while the REST client uses HTTP protocols to access and modify the resources. URIs, which are global IDs, are used to identify the resources. To represent resources such as text, XML and JSON, there are various representations used by REST, but the most popular one is JSON.

How to Create a RESTful for a Library

Consider a scenario where you have the JSON database having the users given below in a file:

usernames.json:

```
{
"first_user" : {
"name" : "john",
"password" : "johnpassword",
"profession" : administrator"",
"id": 1
},
"second_user" : {
"name" : "joel",
"password" : "joelpassword",
"profession" : "programmer",
"id": 2
},
"third_user" : {
"name" : "hellen",
"password" : "third_password",
"profession" : "lecturer",
"id": 3
```

```
}
}
```

Note that each user in the above database is associated with a
name, a password, a profession and a user id.

How to List the users

The following code should be implemented in the file
server.js:

```
var exp = require('express');
var app = express();
var f = require("fs");
app.get('/listUsers', function (request, response) {
f.readFile( __dirname + "/" + "usernames.json",
'utf8', function (error, data) {

        console.log( data );
        res.end( data );
});
})


var serv = app.listen(8081, function () {
var host = serv.address().address
var p = serv.address().port
```

```
        console.log("The example app is listening at
http://%s:%s", host, p)

})
```

Save the above as **_server.js_**. We have implemented the REStful API named "listUsers", which normally shows the list of all users in a database. This has been implemented in the line "app.get('/listUsers', function (request, response) { but the code itself for this has been created in a file named "server.js".Once you have done that, on your local machine, open the browser, and then type the following URL:

http://127.0.0.1:8081/userslist

The above URL should give you the following result:

```json
{
"first_user" : {
"name" : "john",
"password" : "johnpassword",
"profession" : administrator"",
"id": 1
},
"second_user" : {
"name" : "joel",
"password" : "joelpassword",
"profession" : "programmer",
"id": 2
},
"third_user" : {
"name" : "hellen",
"password" : "third_password",
"profession" : "lecturer",
"id": 3
}
}
}
```

Once you have put the solution in a production environment, you can choose to modify the IP address.

Adding a User

In this section, you will be shown how to use an API to add a user to the list. The following shows the details for the user who is to be added to the list:

```
user = {
  "fourth_user" : {
    "name" : "Carren",
    "password" : "carrenpassword",
    "profession" : "lawyer",
    "id": 4
  }
}
```

The API for adding a new user to the database should be as follows:

```
var exp = require('express');
var app = express();
var f = require("fs");
var user = {
"fourth_user" : {
        "name" : "Carren",
        "password" : "carrenpassword",
        "profession" : "lawyer",
        "id": 4
}
}
app.get('/addUser', function (req, res) {
// begin by reading the existing users.
f.readFile( __dirname + "/" + "users.json", 'utf8',
function (error, data) {

data = JSON.parse( data );
data["fourth_user"] = user["fourth_user"];
        console.log( data );
res.end( JSON.stringify(data));
});
})
var serv = app.listen(8081, function () {
var host = serv.address().address
```

```
var p = serv.address().port
    console.log("The example app is listening at
http://%s:%s", host, p)

})
```

You can see from the above code that the RESTful API has
been named "addUser". You can save the above API as
saveUsers on your local machine, open the browser and
navigate to the following URL:

http://127.0.0.1:8081/saveUsers

Once you type the above URL, hit the Return key and you will
get the following result:

```
{
"first_user" : {
"name" : "john",
"password" : "johnpassword",
"profession" : administrator"",
"id": 1
},
"second_user" : {
"name" : "joel",
"password" : "joelpassword",
"profession" : "programmer",
"id": 2
},
"third_user" : {
"name" : "hellen",
"password" : "third_password",
"profession" : "lecturer",
"id": 3
}
"fourth_user" : {
"name" : "Carren",
"password" : "carrenpassword",
"profession" : "lawyer",
"id": 4
}
}
```

Showing the Details

Now create an API in which you pass the ID of a particular user and be able to get back their details. The following is the code for the API:

```
var exp = require('express');
var app = express();
var f = require("fs");
app.get('/:id', function (request, response) {
// begin by reading the existing users.
f.readFile( __dirname + "/" + "usernames.json", 'utf8', function (error, d) {

d = JSON.parse( d );
var user = usernames["user" + request.params.id]
        console.log( user );
res.end( JSON.stringify(user));
});
})
var serv = app.listen(8081, function () {
var host = serv.address().address
var p = serv.address().port
        console.log("The example app is listening at http://%s:%s", host, p)
})
```

Once you have written the above code into your file, type the following URL:

http://127.0.0.1:8081/3

With the above URL, you want to get the third user in the list. The following details should be presented to you:

```
{
"name" : "hellen",
"password" : "third_password",
"profession" : "lecturer",
"id": 3
}
```

The main logic lies in the two lines of code:

**var user = usernames["user" + request.params.id]
console.log(user);**

In the first line of the above, we have used the id of the user so as to get their details. The variable "user" has been defined to represent this. This variable has then been used to print the user details on the console. Note that each of the users in the database has their unique id, and this is why it is the only best parameter for use to query their details.

Deleting a User

Create an API that will be used to delete a user from the list. You will have to provide the ID of the user and this user will then be deleted from the database. To delete the user whose ID is 3. Follow the code given below:

```
var exp = require('express');
var app = express();
var f = require("fs");
var id = 3;
app.get('/delUser', function (request, response) {
// Begin by reading the existing users.
f.readFile( __dirname + "/" + "usernames.json", 'utf8', function (error, data) {

data = JSON.parse( data );
delete data["user" + 3];
        console.log( data );
res.end( JSON.stringify(data));
});
})
var serv = app.listen(8081, function () {
var host = serv.address().address
var p = serv.address().port

        console.log("The example app is listening at http://%s:%s", host, p)
```

```
})
```

Now, call the service created above. Open your browser, and then type the following URL:

http://127.0.0.1:8081/delUser

The above should give you the following result:

```
{
"first_user" : {
"name" : "john",
"password" : "johnpassword",
"profession" : administrator"",
"id": 1
},
"second_user" : {
"name" : "joel",
"password" : "joelpassword",
"profession" : "programmer",
"id": 2
},
```

As shown in the above figure, the *third_user* is not in the list since the user has been deleted. We created a variable named "id" and its value has been initialized to a 3, which represents the user with that id in the database.

Chapter 10- Events in Node.js

With the concept of callbacks and events in Node.js, concurrency control is highly supported. The **async** function is used for this purpose. Note that each of the APIs in Node.js is asynchronous and single threaded. The observer pattern is also used. An event loop is kept by the Node thread, and once a task has been completed, the corresponding events are fired and this acts as a signal for the event to be executed.

Event Driven Programming in Node.js

Events that are highly supported in Node.js are responsible for the faster nature of the Node.js technology when compared to other technologies. Once the Node server has been started, the variables are initiated, functions are declared, and the last step is to wait for the events to occur.

When it comes to the concept of event-driven programming, an event loop is used for listening to the events, and whenever an event is detected, a callback function is executed. The *event* module and the *EventEmitter* class in Node.js are used as follows:

```
// Importing the events module
var events = require('events');
// Creating an object of the eventEmitter
var eventEmitter = new events.EventEmitter();
```

For you to bind an event handler with an event, the following syntax is used:

```
// Binding an event and an event handler as follows
eventEmitter.on('eventName', eventHandler);
```

For you to fire an event in a programmatic manner, use the following syntax:

```
// Firing an event
eventEmitter.emit('eventName');
```

To demonstrate how events and EventEmitter can be used in Node.js, create a new file and give it the name *file.js*. Add the following code to the file:

```
// Importing the events module
var evs = require('events');
// Creating an object of the eventEmitter
var evsEmitter = new evs.EventEmitter();
```

```
// Creating an event handler as follows
var conHandler = function connected() {
        console.log('The connection was successful.');
// Firing the data_received event
evsEmitter.emit('data_received');
}
// Binding the connection event with a handler
evsEmitter.on('connection', conHandler);
// Binding the data_received event with an
anonymous function
evsEmitter.on('data_received', function(){

        console.log('The data was received
successfully.');

});
// Firing the connection event
evsEmitter.emit('connection');
        console.log("The Program has Ended.");
```

Once you have added the above code to the file, run it by executing the following command on the terminal:

node file.js

Once you have executed the above command, you should get
the following output:

```
The connection succesful.
The data was received succesfully.
The Program has Ended.
```

To use the Node.js events, create an object of the
eventsEmitter() function. The event handler should be created
from the "connected ()" function.

The Functionality of Node Applications

In Node applications, async functions are used for acceptance of callback functions as the first parameter. Once this has been done, the callback function accepts the error as its first parameter. To demonstrate how this can be done see the example below.

Begin by creating a text file and give it the name *textfile.txt*. Add the following content to the file:

Streams are a kind of objects and with them you can read from a certain source or write to a certain destination. This can be done in a continuous manner.

Create a new JS file and give it the name *file.js*. Add the following code to the file:

```
var f = require("fs");
f.readFile('input.txt', function (error, d) {
if (error){
        console.log(error.stack);
return;
}
```

```
        console.log(d.toString());
});
        console.log("The Program has Ended");
```

Note that an asynchronous function named *"f.readFile()"* was used, which will read the file specified. However, it is possible that an error will occur while performing the read operation. In this case, the object **error** will have the error; otherwise, it will have the contents of the file specified to read. The parameter **error** and **d** will be passed to the callback function by **readFile()** method once the operation for reading the file has completed, and finally, the contents of the file will be printed out.

Now that you have added the above code to the file, run it by executing the following command:

node file.js

The command given above should give the following result once executed:

The Program has ended

Streams are a kind of objects and with them, one can read from a certain source

or write to a certain destination and this can be done in a continuous manner.

Chapter 11- Node.js Packaging

The code for Node.js is open and can be copied the way you would copy normal JavaScript code. However, this is not possible for now. A new project, named *JXcor*, which is open source, has introduced a new and unique feature that can be used for packaging and encryption of the source files and some of the other assets into JX packages.

Consider a situation in which a project has numerous files. The work of distribution of this project can be made easier by use of the JXcore project since you will be able to package all of these files into a single package.

Installation of JXcore

This is easy. It only involves downloading and unpacking the package. To install JXcore on to your system, follow the steps given below:

1. Visit the site http://jxcore.com/downloads/ and then download the JXcore package. Make sure that you download the best edition for your operating system and architecture. If using CentOS 64 bit, execute the following command to download the package:

    ```
    $ wget https://s3.amazonaws.com/nodejx/jx_rh64.zip
    ```

    The above command will download the package **jx_rh64.zip**.

2. The second step involves unpacking the above package. The jx binary file should then be copied into the directory **/usr/bin** or into any other directory of choice depending on how you have set up your system. The following commands can be used for this purpose:

    ```
    $ unzip jx_rh64.zip
    $ cp jx_rh64/jx /usr/bin
    ```

3. The next step should involve setting up of the **PATH** variable correctly, so that jx can be run from anywhere the way you want. Execute the following command:

```
$ export PATH=$PATH:/usr/bin
```

4. Now that the installation should have completed, you should then verify whether it ran successfully. Execute the following simple command on the terminal:

```
$ jx --version
```

If everything executed correctly, you should have the version of the JXcore project printed as the result.

```
v0.10.32
```

Code for Packaging

Suppose that you have kept the files for your project in different directories within your machine, including the *index.js* file for Node.js, which is the main file. Your intention is to package the project. In this case, you have to navigate to the directory, and then execute the following jx command:

```
$ jx package index.js index
```

The entry file for the Node.js project is the file *index.js*. In the command above, *index.js was used* to keep the main file for the project name the same. The command will then package everything for the project, and you will notice that it forms two files, which include the following:

- **index.jxp** - this file will contain the complete details of the project that are needed for compilation of the project.

- **index.js** - this file is in binary form and is ready for shipping into a production environment.

How to Launch the JX file

Suppose the original project for Node.js was executing as shown below:

```
$ node index.js command_line_arguments
```

Once you have used JXcore to package your project, you can then start it by use of the following command:

```
$ jx index.jx command_line_arguments
```

This JXcore can be used for packaging of Node.js applications.

Conclusion

It can be concluded that Node.js is a platform that was developed in the JavaScript engine. It runs on the server side of applications, making it easy for network applications to scale efficiently and effectively. The I/O mechanism this platform relies on is lightweight and event-driven. Due to the open-source nature of the platform, you can access and download it onto your systems for free. If your application will operate on large amounts of data and in a real-time manner, then this is the platform for you to use.

This platform can be used on different operating systems, provided you download the best version for the platform in terms of type and architecture. The platform also comes with a library, which acts as a web server on its own. This shows how advantaged the users of this platform are. When you need to use a web server for your application, you will not have to install a web server from an external environment, such as the HTTP web server you can use the in-built web server for the platform.

To use Node.js on your local system, you must have an editor and the binary installable for the platform have to be installed into the system. It is after you have assembled these that you can get into programming. When it comes to the text editor, you can choose the one of your choice such as Notepad, EMACs or VIM. In the case of Linux and Mac OS X, you have to use the command line to extract the package that you downloaded. Installation of this in Windows is much easier as you only have to follow the on-screen instructions that are presented to you.

The Node.js platform offers the REPL terminal, which you can use to perform the various tasks including mathematical operations. You now know how to use these and you will become a Node.js expert.

www.ingramcontent.com/pod-product-compliance
Lightning Source LLC
Chambersburg PA
CBHW061013050326
40689CB00012B/2633